To our families and friends,
and our "kids" at Martin School,
South San Francisco, California,
for their endless support and
enthusiasm.

Pat and Rosemary

The Kid's Party Book

Patricia Barrett and Rosemary Dalton
Spot illustrations by Patricia Barrett
Full page art by Young Artists

A Nitty Gritty Book*
Published by
Nitty Gritty Productions
P.O. Box 5457
Concord, California 94524

*Nitty Gritty Books -- Trademark
Owned by Nitty Gritty Productions
Concord, California

ISBN 0-911954-44-9

Library of Congress Catalog Card Number: 77-82344

Contents

Happy
Birthday

Hi Party-Planners and Party-Goers,

This party book is full of all kinds of ideas for you and your parents. Planning your party can be as much fun as having the party - especially if it's your birthday or a special family holiday.

Start your plans early so that you have time to get everything ready. This book has lots of ideas for invitations, decorations, menus, recipes you can cook yourself, and party games. There are 16 parties planned for you, but we hope you will look through this book and mix and match the things you like the best. Using your imagination, and deciding what you like is half the fun of party planning.

This book also has lots of holiday recipes, decorations, and craft ideas, so that you can be creative and help make your family's holidays special.

Note: Most parties have a menu. Recipes you can make are starred* in the menus.

Planning Ahead for Your Party

If your party is well planned it will go smoothly and be lots of fun. Here are some party planning tips for you.

1 Discuss your party planning ideas with your family. Get their permission and their help. One of the things you will need to decide together is how much you can spend on your party, and what kind of party it will be.

2. Decide on the number of guests you want to invite to your party and whether you want an indoor or an outdoor party. If you are having a lot of guests an outdoor party would

probably be best, but make sure you have enough room to hold the party indoors in case of bad weather. It really will help, regardless of the size of your party, to have an adult or older friend help supervise.

3. Plan your party on paper about three weeks before it's going to happen. Write down the date, time of day, and the guest list. If you pick a party theme or central idea, it will help set the mood of your party, and give you ideas for decorations, invitations, things to eat, and games or

things to do.

4. If you give yourself plenty of time you can make many of your party props yourself or with your family and friends. Many party decorations and invitations are available in stores too, but making things yourself will help keep your party within your budget. Being creative can be lots of fun too.

4. Have an idea what the order of your party will be. One easy party plan for a birthday celebration would be to open gifts first, eat, and then play games. Vary the sequence to suit yourself. If

you are having a lunch or a dinner party, you would probably plan to have refreshments first (something to drink), and then the meal. Then you could open presents (if it is a present opening party) and have games.

Plan several games for your party, with prizes if you like. It's a good idea to plan more games than you think you need, in case of extra time. You may want to have "loot bags" for your guests to use to take home party favors, prizes or other party things. Lunch bags, with guests names on them, are good "loot bags".

On the Day of Your Party...

Remember, Party Day is Camera Day!

1 Have everything ready before your guests arrive. Have the table set, decorations up, game materials all set up, and food ready to go. Have a camera loaded with film too. It's great to have pictures of your party! To get all these preparations done you have to start the night before or early in the morning.

2. Be dressed and ready before your guests arrive. It is very important to greet your guests at the door. Try to make them feel welcome. Hang up their coats or sweaters. (You may need adult help for this.) Then thank your friends for the gifts (if they have brought

you some). Stack your presents in the special place where you will be opening them.

3. Introduce your friends if they do not know each other. When all your guests have arrived, begin your party in the sequence you have planned. Make sure that everyone has a "loot bag" for prizes and party favors to take home.

4. When you open each party gift, thank your friend. Tuck the card in the gift so that when you are writing your thank you notes you can remember who gave you which gift. Put your gifts away after you

open them and plan to play with them after your friends are gone. This way no one gets hurt feelings over which present you like the best.

5. When your party is over, thank your friends and say good-by to them at the door. And now its

6. CLEAN-UP TIME! Be sure to help! It's a good idea to have large plastic bags for party litter.

7. Remember to write notes to your friends, thanking them for the party gifts they brought you.

Party Planning Checklist

Here is a list that will help you plan your party without forgetting something important (like your birthday cake!)

1. Plan your party theme, date, and time.
2. Make or buy invitations.  Mail them or give them to your friends.
3. Make and set up decorations and party favors.
4. Decide on a menu. Prepare the party food.
5. Plan games or things to do. Have game equipment ready.
6. Have a large litter bag ready for clean-up.

How to Trace Invitations

You can buy party invitations or make your own. We have included several traceable invitations in this book. To trace an invitation lay tracing paper on top and tape it. 1. Trace around the outline. Snip the tape with a scissors to free the pattern. 2. To transfer the pattern to firmer paper, go over the back of the pattern with soft pencil lines. 3. Then put the drawing (soft pencil side down) on the paper you wish to use. Go over the lines on the right side of the tracing paper with a hard pencil. The imprint will come off on the good paper. Like magic!

Tracing the invitation.

Soft pencil on back of tracing.

Drawing over tracing with hard pencil.

Other Invitations or Birthday Cards

You may want to make your own invitations or cards without using a pattern. To do this you can fold paper several ways and then decorate it with cut paper, lettering, crayons, marking pens, fabric, paint- whatever you like. Here are some ways to fold paper for your own unique cards:

①

②
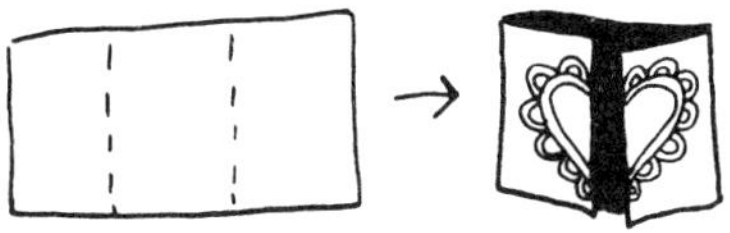

③
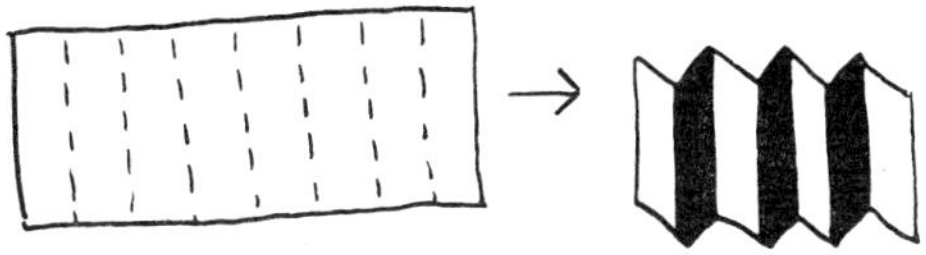

④
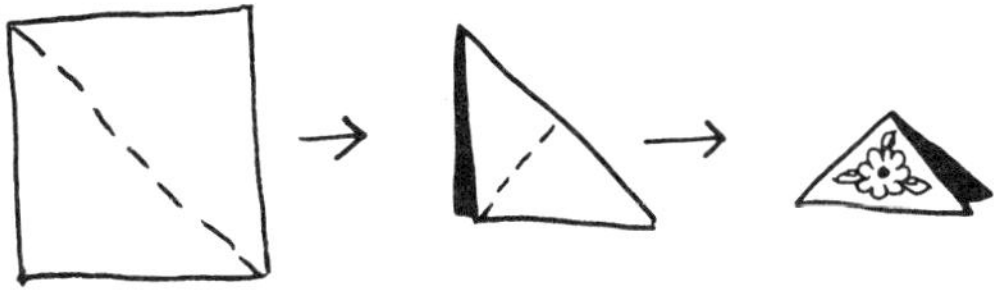

⑤
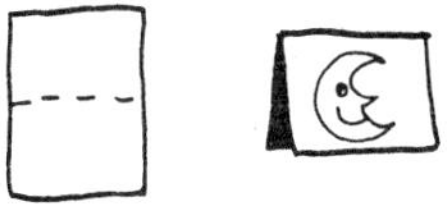

See what you can invent.

How to Make Envelopes

You can buy envelopes for your invitations or make your own. Envelopes must be at least $3\frac{1}{2}$ by 4 inches in size to be sent through the mail. Make sure your envelopes are this size or larger.

Follow these directions to make a simple envelope:
① Fold a piece of paper in half. Lay your card on top.

② Draw around the card, leaving a space about $\frac{1}{4}$ inch bigger than the card. Cut off the sides.

- cut
- cut

③ Cut off one front edge, but leave the other one to make a flap.

← 1 front edge left for flap.

④ Paste the sides of the envelope together. (About $\frac{1}{4}$ inch on each side). When dry, put your card in and paste the top flap closed.

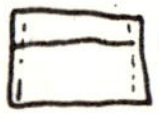
← Pasted edges and top flap.

What to Include in an Invitation

Invitations should be mailed or handed out about 10 days before the party. Your invitations should include the following information:

Kind of party ______________________

Date ______________________

Time it starts and ends ______________________

Lunch, Dinner or Refreshments ______________________

Where it will be ______________________

Name of the party giver ______________________
(and who the party is for)

Address ______________________

Phone ______________________

Please respond ______________________

Basic Party Decorating Ideas

Party decorations should be bright and colorful. You can hang decorations from the ceiling or put them on walls. Balloons add lots of color. By rubbing them on your clothing for a minute you create static electricity. Then when you put the balloons against the wall they will stay there!

Cakes or cupcakes are a good centerpiece for a party. Use a party tablecloth, or make your own with layers of one or two colors of crepe paper. Plastic placemats are also good. Colored paper plates and cups, and plastic spoons and forks add to the table decor too.

Crepe paper streamers are an easy, colorful party decoration. Buy ready-made streamers, or make your own by cutting 2-inch segments across a package of crepe paper. Hang streamers from the ceiling, over doorways and windows – even across your party table. Be careful not to hang streamers near a light. This could cause a fire!

Another way to hang streamers is to twist them as you hang them. Or put 2 colors of crepe paper together, then twist. Hang balloons and other party decorations from them if you like.

Place Cards and Party Favors

Place cards show your friends where to sit at your party table. Fold construction paper in half, the size you want your card to be.

Decorate the front of the card with a small picture or your friend's name.

To make another easy kind of place card poke a lolli-pop or name sign into a cupcake or paper cup. Or write your friends' names on paper plates with icing in a tube.

You can also make people or an-imal place cards from construction paper. Make tabs and fold them back so the card can stand.

Place Cards and Party Favors (cont.)

Ice cream cones make great party favors. Write your friends' names on the cones with icing in a tube. Then fill each cone with candy, nuts or other treats.

You can buy nut cups to hold nuts and candy , or make your own party baskets. Take a piece of paper the size you want your basket to be. Seven by 7 inches is a good size. Cut slits in each corner.  Fold the ends up and staple each side. Add a handle, decorations, and a name if you like. Fill the baskets with party goodies.

Place Cards and Party Favors (cont.)

You need:
Small cardboard tubes
Crepe paper or tissue paper
Ribbon or yarn
Candy, nuts, raisins, small toys, whatever you like.

Cut pieces of crepe or tissue paper about 6 inches wider than the tube, and long enough to wrap around the tube. Lay a tube down on a piece of paper. Wrap and tie one end.

Fill the open end with whatever you like. Attach names if you want to use these favors as place cards. Fun party surprises!

Party Hats

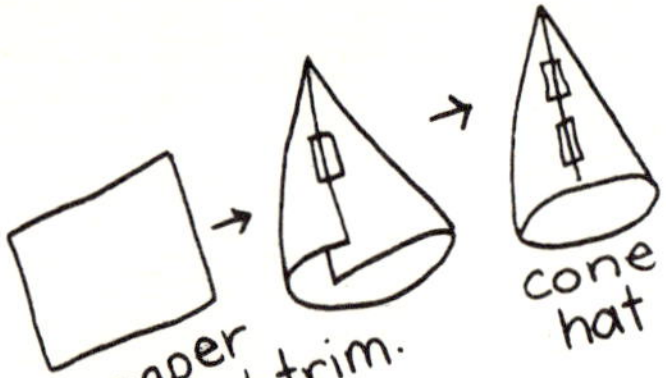

Roll paper
Tape and trim.

cone hat

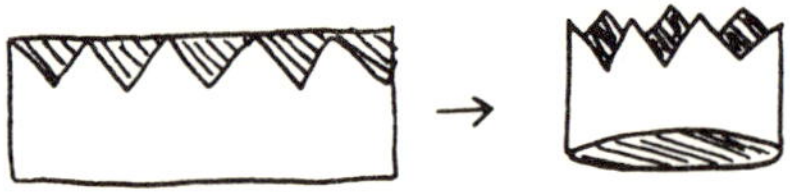

crown

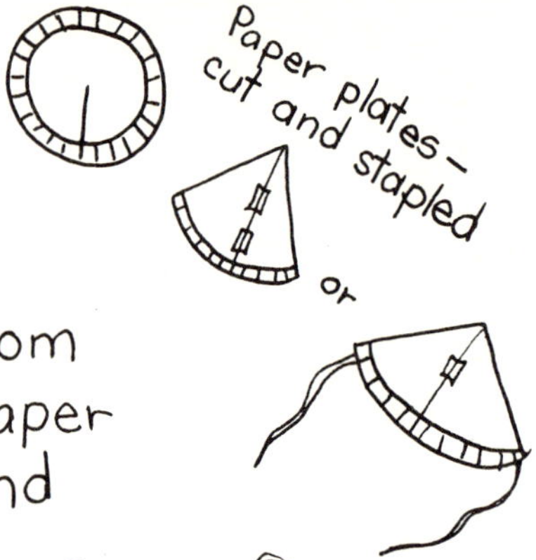

Paper plates - cut and stapled

or

Party hats can be made from many things - construction paper, paper plates, newspaper, paper strips and all kinds of scraps.

cone

\+

hat brim

Cut a cone with flaps
Attach brim.

Make brim wide or narrow - depending on type of hat.

Paper strip for headband

crown + hearts

Add bows, fringe, hearts, flowers, feathers - whatever you want to add.

Cake and Cupcake Decorating Tips

The easiest way to frost cupcakes or cake is to use a spatula.  Be sure your cake is cool. If you really want to make the job easier, put the cake in the freezer for a while, then frost it.

To make clean-up easy when frosting a cake (and to keep from frosting the cake plate too!) put 3 pieces of overlapping wax paper under your cake.  When you are finished frosting, just pull the paper out, and you have a clean plate!

It's fun to make a drawing on a cake! Just freeze the cake, then frost in a background color. "Draw" with a toothpick, then go over your lines with different colors of frosting tubes. This will look great!

About Birthday Parties

Many of the parties in this book are written as holiday parties or specialized parties rather than birthday celebrations. Any of these can easily be made into birthday parties by adding a birthday cake or cupcakes. Then remember to mention on your invitations that your party is for a birthday.

Once you have read this book and know more about setting up parties, you can plan other kinds of parties easily, around any theme you like. Just pick a theme and choose recipes and games that go with it. Here is a list of party themes to stimulate your imagination.

List of Party Themes

- Space
- Robots
- Circus
- Pirates
- Hobos
- Magic
- Kites
- Dolls
- Pets
- Zoo
- Indians

- April Fool's Day
- Camping, Hikes
- Gardening
- Zodiac Signs
- Cooking
- Play Dough
- Crafts Projects
- Sports
- Overnight
- Cartoon Characters
- Cooky-Making

- Plays - Writing and giving
- Puppet Shows, puppet making
- Japanese Tea Party
- St. Patrick's Day
- Chinese New Years
- Fourth of July
- Mexican Fiesta
- Pasta Party - Italian theme
- International Party
- And anything else you can think of...

Carnival
Party
super

Carnival Party

Adult help needed for this party.

This party is like a real carnival, with booths, prizes, and good things to eat. You need adults, or older kids to help you run each booth you set up. This party is best held outdoors, or in the garage or basement.

How to Set Up Booths

There are several ways to make simple booths. One way is to put a broom or mop handle between two chairs or cardboard cartons.
Hang an old sheet, crepe paper, or decorated cardboard sign on the handle.

How to Set Up Booths (cont.)

A different kind of booth is made from a card table or another small table. You can also use a large cardboard carton or cartons taped together. This booth gives you counter space. Decorate your booths with balloons or streamers. Make signs to hang from your counter or above your booths to advertise what games can be played.

Carnival Party Invitation

Fold a piece of paper in half.  Trace the clown on one half. Decorate your invitation with marking pens, crayons, paints or fabric scraps. If you like, do each invitation differently.

You could also cut your clown out, leaving it joined at the hat

or hair.

Clown Make-Up Booth

You won't believe how different make-up can make you look. You need an adult "make-up" person to make you and your friends look like clowns. Here is

You need:

- An adult or older kid
- Cold cream
- Water Soluble Masquerade make-up – red, white, and black
- (Hypo-allergenic make-up is best, in case of sensitive skin)
- Lipstick, rouge, eyebrow pencils, make-up crayons
- Add-ons if you like: noses, glasses, mustaches
- Old shirt to wear while make-up is being applied.

Clown Make-Up Booth (cont.)

how to apply clown make-up, one person at a time: First cover the face with cold cream. This will make the make-up easy to take off later. Next moisten fingertips with water and spread white make-up over the face and chin. Use black for eyebrows, red for noses and mouths. Thin black lines are good for outlining features, or large areas of color such as a clown's mouth. To take off make-up use lots of cold cream and wipe it with tissue. Then wash with soap and water and you are back to your old self. Ugh!

Popcorn Booth
Guess How Many Kernels Game Too...

A popcorn booth is great for nibbling! Make a booth with a counter top. Pop popcorn ahead of time and put it in paper bags or paper cups. Let your friends help themselves! Munch, munch....

Guess How Many Kernels

Put a jar filled with popcorn kernels on your booth counter-top. Count the kernels ahead of time and tape the number on the bottom of the jar. Let friends guess the amount by putting their names and guesses in a box. Closest guesser wins a prize!

Wet Sponge Throw

Willing volunteers needed! Lots of fun!

To set up this game you need a booth with an old sheet, plastic cloth, or oilcloth hanging behind it. An old shower curtain (or even a large piece of cardboard ) will work too. Cut a hole in the cloth or cardboard big enough for a head to stick through.

Find a willing volunteer and let him wear an old raincoat or plastic garbage bag 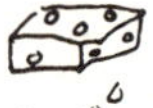 — with head and armholes cut out. This will keep your victim semi-dry. Have a pail of water with wet sponges. Give each person a few chances to hit the target. Give a prize for the person who scores the most "soggy" hits. Your volunteer deserves something too!

Penny Pitch
Beanbag Throw Too...

To set up a penny pitch game put a lot of old plates and cups on cardboard boxes a few feet behind your booth counter. Have a small prize on each cup or plate. Give each guest the same number of pennies to throw. If a penny lands on a plate or in a cup, the tosser gets the prize.

Beanbag Throw

Stack paper cups on a box. Let guests each have 3 tries to knock <u>all</u> the cups down. Winners get prizes!

Carnival Party Menu

Ice Cream Clowns

For each clown put a scoop of ice cream on a plate. Add a sugar cone hat. Decorate with candies – chocolate bits, red hots, jelly beans, gum drops. Make hair with icing-in-a-tube or prepared whipping cream.

Hot Dog Booth

Boil enough water to cover your hot dogs. Put hot dogs in the pan. Cover the pan and turn off the heat. Let the hot dogs sit in the covered pan

for 5 minutes. Then put them in buns. Wrap them in foil and keep them in the oven until you are ready to put them in your booth. Have mustard, catsup, relish and paper plates at your hot dog booth. Let your friends help themselves. Serve pink lemonade with the hot dogs.

Fang Lady
Monster Party
Wolfman

Monster Party

When you send out your party invitations, ask your friends to come as their favorite monster. Some ideas are: Frankenstein, Dracula, Wolfman, King Kong, Godzilla, Were-Wolf, Mummy, The Fly, Vampire, The Bride of Frankenstein, or your own creepy creation!

Monster Party Invitation

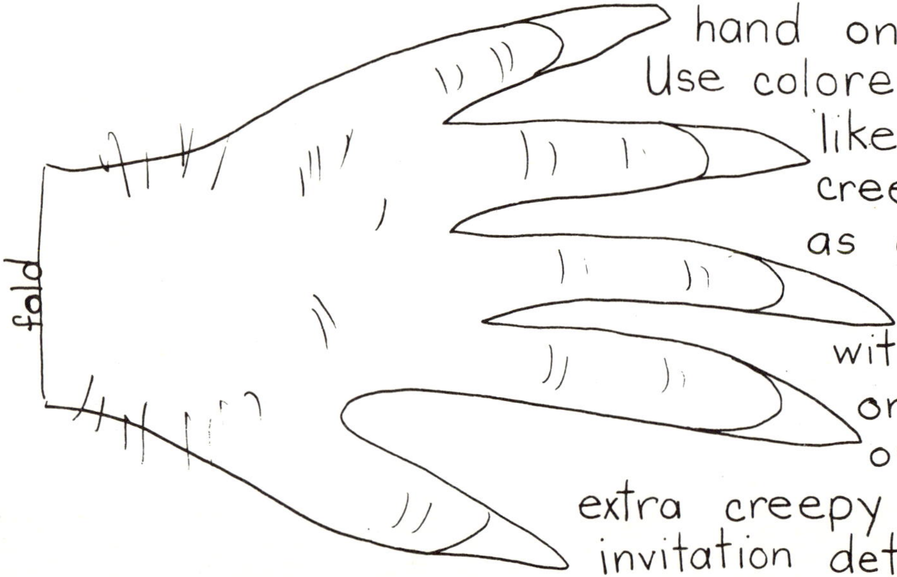

Trace this invitation or trace around your own hand on folded paper. Use colored paper if you like. Then add creepy details such as green claws, hair or scars with marking pen or crayon. Glue on yarn for an extra creepy invitation. Write invitation details inside.

Monster Party Decorations and Menu

Monster cut-outs are great decorations for your monster party. Just lay down on a large sheet of brown wrapping paper and have someone trace around you. Cut out the outline and paint or color it to look like your favorite monster! Make several with friends and put them on the wall near your party table. Creepy!

Monster Cakes

To make Monster Cakes mix up your favorite cake recipe or cake mix. Pour the batter into lined cupcake pans. Bake according to directions. Let cool and frost with frosting mix or a good frosting recipe.

You need:
- Cake mix or favorite recipe
- Frosting mix or recipe
- Cupcake pan and cupcake papers
- Small plastic monsters

Now you are ready for the Monster part– Put a small plastic monster (available in dime stores) on top of each cupcake. Your friends will love them!

Spooketti

Adult help may be needed.

To make this Monster-type spaghetti really fun to eat, serve it in banana split dishes or an ice cream parfait glass. For this recipe you need:

- 1/4 cup chopped onion
- 1/4 cup salad or olive oil
- 1 pound ground beef
- clove of garlic - chopped
- 4-ounce can mushrooms
- 2 cups canned tomatoes
- 1-8 ounce can tomato sauce
- 1-6 ounce can tomato paste

- 1 teaspoon salt
- 1/4 teaspoon oregano
- 1/4 teaspoon pepper
- 1/8 teaspoon basil
- 1/8 teaspoon thyme

1 pound package spaghetti
grated cheese

Spookettí (cont.)

Chop $\frac{1}{4}$ cup of onions. Put $\frac{1}{4}$ cup of oil into a large frying pan. Slowly fry onions on low heat until they look clear. Add the ground beef, finely chopped garlic, mushrooms, tomatoes, tomato sauce and paste, salt, and spices.

Cook on low heat for 2 hours. Stir once in a while. Cook spaghetti, using directions on package. Drain spaghetti in a colander. Mix cooked spaghetti and sauce. Serve with grated parmesan cheese. Monsters love it!

Monster Swing (Statues) Bat Man's Bluff too.

Half the fun of this game is the funny way Monsters "freeze". A leader spins each Monster by the hand and then lets go. The Monster freezes the way he or she lands.

Bat Man's Bluff

Blindfold one player. Spin him or her around. "It" tries to catch other players and guess who is caught. If "It" guesses correctly (only 3 guesses), the person caught becomes "It", and the game continues.

Pin the Fangs on Dracula

This game is a variation of "Pin the Tail on the Donkey". Draw and color a large picture of Dracula, and hang it on the wall. Cut out fangs (big teeth). Make one for each player. Each player gets a turn to be blindfolded, spun around, then pin a fang on the picture. The player who comes closest to Dracula's mouth wins the game.

Monster March
(Musical Chairs)

Set up a row of chairs in the middle of a big room. Have every other facing in the opposite direction (frontward , backward , etc.). Ask an adult or older friend to be in charge of starting and stopping some music.

When the music starts all Monsters march around the chairs. When it stops everyone scrambles for a chair. The player with no chair is "out". Remove a chair and continue until there are two players and one chair. The player who gets the last chair wins.

Scavenger
Hunt

Scavenger Hunt

This is a party for good weather. Before the party, prepare a list of about 10 things you want your guests to find in the neighborhood. It's a good idea to talk to your neighbors ahead of time! Give your guests a list of neighbors who would not mind being called on by scavengers!

When guests arrive, divide them into teams of 3 or 4, depending on how many people you invite. Give each team a different area to cover (and a list of houses or apartments they can call on).

Scavenger Hunt (cont.)

Give each team a list of things to find, and a paper bag. Set a half hour to 1 hour time limit. The team that comes back with the most items wins.

One of the most exciting things about planning this party is making up your list of things to find. Ask your family and friends for ideas. About 10 ideas are enough for a list. Give teams different lists or the same ones. Some suggested ideas are:

1951 penny
2 red beans
rubber spider
paper clip
seashell
star macaroni ✡
4-holed button
wooden spool
used sandpaper
cigar band
red lollipop
1-cent stamp

Scavenger Hunt Invitation

Trace this invitation on white or grey paper. Color it grey and black. Cut it out and fold it. Add the eyes so your friends will lift the lid and be surprised. Write invitation inside.

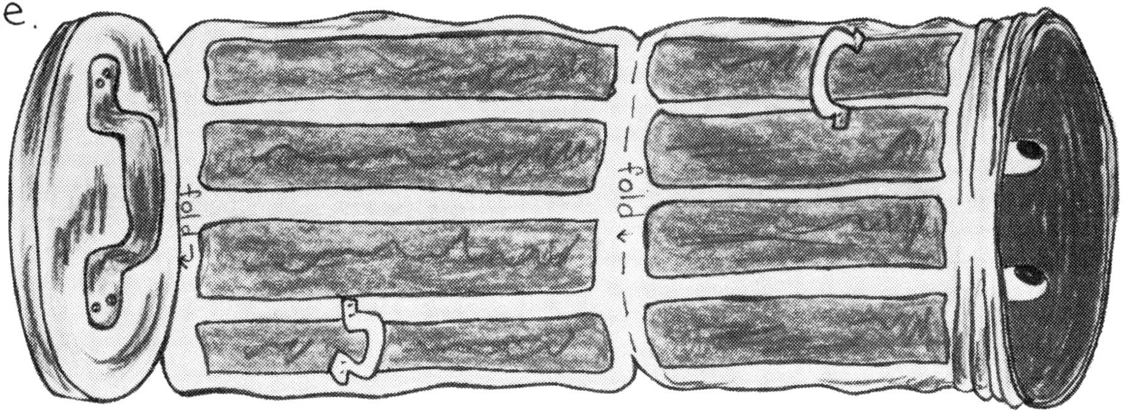

Scavenger Hunt Decorations and Menu

Some people call "junk" or things they just can't use "white elephants". Since you are going to be scavenging this kind of item it might be fun to decorate with cut-outs of white elephants.

Submarine Sandwiches

You need:

All kinds of lunch meats such as salami, bologna, cheese, turkey, ham, mortadella - your favorites.

Large loaf of French bread or small hard rolls.

Relish, pickles, mustard, mayonnaise.

Slice open the French bread or rolls.  Get adult help if necessary.

Spread mayonnaise, mustard or butter (or a combination) on the bread. Add the lunch meats. Spread more mayonnaise or mustard between the layers of lunch meat for a super juicy sandwich.

Slice, but not all the way through.  Wrap in foil or plastic wrap, and take this sandwich anywhere. Serves 5 good eaters.

Rainbow Cake

You need:
2 boxes of white cake mix
4 round layer cake pans
food coloring
3 half pints whipped cream
powdered sugar
vanilla

Mix the cakes according to the package directions. Separate batter into 4 bowls. Pick 4 colors for your cake layers. Add food coloring, 1 drop at a time, to each bowl of cake batter until you get the 4 colors you want. Bake cakes according to the directions. Remove layers from the pan when cool. Frost with whipped cream frosting (p. 53). Put sliced bananas between layers for a yummy treat!

Whipped Cream Frosting

Put 3 half pints of whipping cream into a deep bowl. Add 1 teaspoon vanilla and 3-6 tablespoons of powdered sugar. Beat with an egg beater or electric mixer. (Get adult help if necessary). Beat whipping cream until it is thick enough for frosting. (Don't beat it too long - you will have sweet butter!)

Frost one layer of your cake at a time, placing one layer on top of another. Then frost the outside of the cake. When you cut this cake your guests are in for a surprise!

SODA
FOUNTAIN
PARTY

Soda Fountain Party

This is a do-it-yourself party, where your guests make their own concoctions. Adult help is needed. You will probably need some of the following basic ingredients:

Large paper cups (for sodas)

Paper bowls (for sundaes and banana splits)

3 flavors of ice cream—vanilla, strawberry and chocolate are good choices.

Straws, plastic spoons

Soda Fountain Party (cont.)

Other things you will need for this party are:

3 ice cream scoops
Syrups and toppings- a variety of flavors
Napkins, towels
Marshmallow cream sauce
Chopped nuts, prepared whipped cream, cherries
Bananas
Coke, Seven-Up, Rootbeer, plain soda (carbonated water).
Balloons for decorations.

Your guests may need a little help deciding what to make. You may want to show them how to make a banana split, sundae, and soda.

Soda Fountain Party Invitation

To make invitations for your Soda Fountain Party, draw an ice cream cone (or other ice cream concoction) on the front of folded paper.  Write party information inside. Or trace, cut out, and color the pattern below. Write details inside the cone.

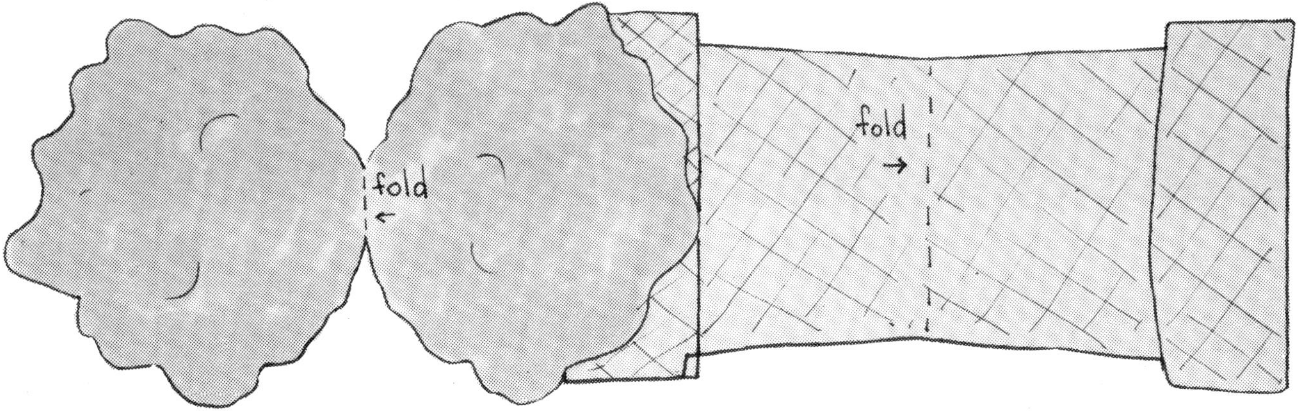

How to Make a Banana Split

To make a banana split you need one ripe banana split in half lengthwise.  You need 3 scoops of ice cream - one vanilla, one chocolate, and one strawberry. Put the banana in a bowl or banana split dish. Put the ice cream on top, and add 3 different flavored toppings - strawberry, pineapple and chocolate. Top with whipped cream, chopped nuts and a marashino cherry. Vary this any way you like. Dig in!

How to Make a Sundae
Black and White Sundae

You need one scoop of vanilla ice cream and one scoop of chocolate. Put them in a bowl or a sundae dish. Cover the chocolate ice cream with marshmallow cream sauce. Cover the vanilla ice cream with chocolate sauce. Top everything with whipped cream and cherries and nuts.

To make other kinds of sundaes, experiment with ice creams and sauces.

How to Make a Soda

Chocolate Soda

Put 2 or 3 teaspoons of chocolate or vanilla ice cream and chocolate syrup (2 or 3 teaspoons) in the bottom of a tall glass. Blend thoroughly with a long-handled spoon. Add enough carbonated water (plain soda) to fill the glass $\frac{3}{4}$ full. 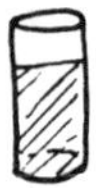 Then add a large scoop of vanilla or chocolate ice cream. Top with whipped cream and a cherry.

To make a strawberry soda, use strawberry sauce and a scoop of strawberry ice cream. Have fun experimenting too!

Decorated Ice Cream Cones
Purple Cows, too!

If some of your party guests would like ice cream cones let them scoop up their own creations. If you like, have small bowls of some of the following ingredients to sprinkle on the ice cream: chopped nuts, coconut, small chocolate chips, colored sugar sprinkles, other small candies.

Purple Cow

The name is almost as good as the drink! Loosely fill a glass with vanilla ice cream. Pour root beer into the glass. Terrific!

Unbirthday
Party

Unbirthday Party

If your birthday is on Christmas or another big holiday, you may want to choose another day during the year to celebrate your birthday- an Unbirthday Party! This is just like a birthday party, with presents and cake for you.

Another way to have an Unbirthday Party is to invite friends and celebrate everybody's "Unbirthday." You may want to ask your friends (in the invitation) to bring a small wrapped "grab-bag" gift. Put these gifts in a bag and let everyone reach in for their own surprise present!

Unbirthday Party Invitation

Trace this cake invitation on folded paper  or design your own. Cut out the cake (do not cut the fold) or leave on the paper. Decorate with crayons, paints or marking pens. Make some cakes different if you like. Write your invitation inside the card.

Party Favors and Decorations

Crazy candles (available at party stores) would be fun to put on an Unbirthday Cake or cup-cakes — blow them out and they light themselves again! Your friends won't believe their eyes!

Crowns are a great favor for this party. See p. 22 for directions on making them. Balloons and streamers are easy party decorations too!

Lotsa Little Cakes

You need:
Your favorite cake mix
White frosting mix
Food coloring
Rectangular ▭ cake pan
Cake trims such as: nuts, gum-drops, sugar sprinkles, chocolate bits
Candles

Make your cake according to the directions on the package. Put frosting in 3-4 small bowls. Add a different food coloring to each bowl. (Add it a drop at a time until you get a color you like). Frost the cake with the different colored frostings. Cut it in

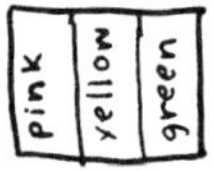

or

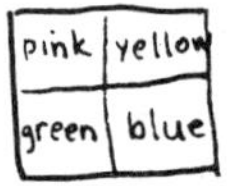

small squares and decorate each little cake with cake trims. Add a candle and it's Happy Unbirthday time!

Surprise Balls

Surprise Balls are made from crepe paper or yarn, with a party favor rolled up inside. Wrap as many surprises in the ball as you like.

Start your ball by wrapping a party favor in cut crepe paper strips or yarn. Continue wrapping until the ball is the size you want. If you add more than one surprise wrap them several layers apart. Tape the end of the ball and write your friend's name on it. Good favors are rings, toy cars, whistles, toy spiders, tiny dolls, candies - look in the dime store for ideas.

aloha!
Luau
COCOA-
NUTS

Luau
Candy leis too!

A luau can be held indoors or out. Good decorations would be nets, strings of seashells, real or artificial flowers, driftwood, leis. Polynesian posters would be good too.

Candy Leis

Candy leis are a great party favor. To make them you need all kinds of wrapped candies. (Wrapped gum will work too.) Tie the candy and gum together with pieces of ribbon.

Luau Invitation

Trace this luau invitation on folded paper. Use white or yellow paper. Color your invitations with paint, crayons or marking pens so that it looks like a pineapple. Write the invitation inside the card.

Paper Leis

Make leis ahead for your Luau, or let your friends make their own as part of the party fun. You need crepe paper streamers of assorted colors. (Or cut your own from crepe paper). 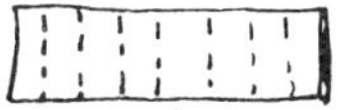 Thread a large needle with heavy thread about 64 inches long. Knot one end of the thread. Sew through the center of the crepe paper strip with a running stitch.  After you have stitched a little, gather the paper back to the knot and twist it loosely. Keep going until your thread is filled. Tie the ends of the crepe paper together and put on your lei. Aloha!

Drop the Lei
(Drop the Handkerchief)

Have your friends make a circle. The player who is "It" walks outside the circle holding a paper lei. "It" drops the lei behind someone and runs. That player picks up the lei and chases "It" around the circle, trying to tag him or her before "It" reaches the empty space.

This game can be varied for different holidays, dropping paper hearts, shamrocks, pumpkins, turkeys, stars, Easter eggs, etc.

Coconut Relay Race

You need 2 teams and a coconut (or ball) for each team. See p.161 for more about relays). The teams line up behind a starting line, with each team leader holding a "coconut". At a signal the leaders race to the finish line, leave the ball or coconut there, and race back. The next players run to get the coconut. They hand it to the next player, who then runs and leaves it at the finish line. First team finished wins. To vary the game, pass the coconut over heads or under legs of team members.

Luau Menu
Surfer Snacks too!

Buy wooden skewers. Thread them with pieces of lunch meats, cheese, pickles, olives, pineapple chunks, little tomatoes, even pieces of cooked hot dog. Put each skewer on a bun. Serve with mustard, catsup, mayonnaise, etc.

Show your friends how to pull out the skewer before eating! Skewers can be threaded a day ahead and stored in refrigerator.

Fruit Ka-bobs

You need:
Wooden skewers
Variety of fresh fruits, such as bananas, apples, cantaloupe, strawberries, oranges, pears.
Canned fruit, such as pine-apple chunks, mandarin oranges, tropical fruit assortment.

Pick a variety of fresh and frozen fruits you like. Try to pick fruits in season. The cost will be more reasonable. Peel and slice the fresh fruit. Drain the canned fruit and save the juice. It will be good added to your Hawaiian punch. Thread the fruit on the skewers and serve.

Outdoor Parties

Outdoor Parties

There are many kinds of parties you can have outdoors: a barbecue, swim, beach party, picnic or hike. If you are having a barbecue you need adult help with the cooking. For a picnic, hike or beach party, prepare food ahead to take with you. You may also need an adult along too.

African Safari Party Invitation

Many parties can be held indoors or out. The Safari Party is one of them.

Trace the hippo invitation or create your own invitation.

If you have this party outdoors a barbecue would be fun.

Decorations and Menu

Pictures of animals and African masks are good decorations for a Safari Party. "Fake fur" place-mats are easy to make. Tear open big paper bags, and tear them placemat size. Color lines, stripes, or spots on the mats. Tear or fringe the edges.

Brownie-Marshmallow Kabobs

Make brownies, using your favorite recipe or mix. Cut them into squares. Thread brownies and marshmallows on skewers (one skewer per person). Heat over barbecue until marshmallows melt. Use pot holders when touching hot skewers. Take off skewers and put on a plate.
Wow! These are good!

Animal Cookie Cake

Make your favorite cake and frost it. Decorate it with animal crackers and green coconut. Add green food coloring (just a drop!) to coconut to turn it green.

Lions and Leopards

Pick 2 players to make a bridge or "trap". Other players get in line and march under the trap. As the players march they clap and chant: "Lions and leopards, lions and leopards hunting at night, lions and leopards, lions and leopards, catch the Game!" At the word "Game", the trap falls and a player is caught. When 2 players are caught they form a second trap. Other players keep marching, clapping, chanting - going through all the traps and trying not to get caught and be a trap.

Overnight Party
Ghost Stories

Overnight Party
Nachos too!

You need all kinds of munchies for an overnight Party – And plans for a good breakfast. Some good snacks are cheese, crackers, fresh fruits, raisins and nuts. Have sandwiches and rolls for the midnight raid!

Nachos

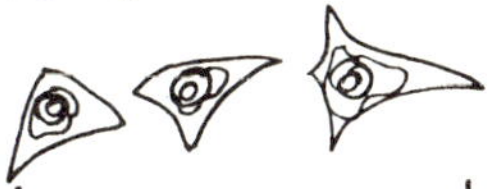

You need king size corn chips, grated cheddar cheese, and Hot Mexican chili peppers, sliced thin. Put one piece of chili on each chip. Sprinkle with cheese. Bake at 400 degrees until the cheese melts. A great snack!

Overnight Party Invitation

Make this invitation like the doorway of your house, or a doorway you like. Fold a piece of paper in half , then in half again. 
Draw and cut a doorway.  Leave the fold uncut so that the door will open. Write the invitation inside and decorate the card.

Banana Pancakes

You need:
- Pancake mix
- Bananas
- Butter
- Syrups, jellies, jams

Mix pancake batter according to the directions on the package. Add 1 sliced banana for each cup of pancake mix. One cup of mix should serve about 6 people. Make pancakes normal size, or silver dollar size. Serve lots of them.

Cook the pancakes according to the directions on the package. Serve them with butter, syrups, jams or jellies. Serve ham or bacon and orange juice to complete the breakfast menu.

HALLOWEEN
Happy
Holloween

Halloween is a great time for costumes and fun. Let your imagination run wild! You can be a ghost, witch, goblin - your favorite monster or cartoon character - or anything else you have ever dreamed of!

Halloween Party Invitation

Fold a piece of white paper in half. Trace the ghost invitation so that the fold is on top.  Cut out the invitation (or leave it on the square of paper if you like). Do not cut the fold.  Write your party information inside the card. You can give ghosts different expressions with different eyes, mouths.

Halloween Decorations

Halloween decorations can be as creepy as you like! A Jack O' Lantern (made from a real pumpkin) is a great decoration - especially with a lighted candle inside. Votive candles in glass containers will not tip.  Get permission for this!

Ghosts, bats, witches and goblins are fun to draw, cut out and hang. You can make a scary ghost by wadding up a newspaper for a head. Put the

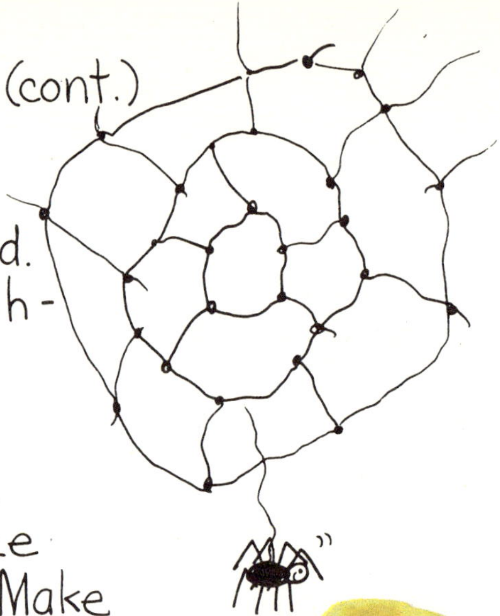

round paper wad in the center of a sheet. Tie the sheet under the wad. Pin on eyes. Hang your ghost with fishing line or string.

Spider webs are another good decoration. Use black or white yarn, cord, or string. Make a circle the size you want your web. Tie it closed. Make other yarn circles inside the first circle. Cut small pieces of yarn and tie one end to the outer circle and one end to the next smallest circle. Keep going until all circles are attached. Hang in creepy place!

Halloween Decorations and Menu

Orange and black crepe paper streamers are easy decorations for your party table or room. Jack O'-Lantern Cake (p. 94) makes a good centerpiece. You can use 12 by 18 inch construction paper for placemats. If you like, cut them in the shape of jack o' lanterns, witches, bats, ghosts or other Halloween ideas. You can make all the placemats the same, or make different ones.

Jack O'Lantern Cake

Looks great on your party table!

You need:

- Cake mix
- Canned or packaged frosting
- Red and yellow food coloring
- Green sugar sprinkles
- Candy bits – candy corn, miniature chocolate bits
- 2 round cake pans

Make your Halloween cake according to the directions on the package. Pour the batter into 2 round cake pans and bake. Mix the frosting. Add a few drops of red and yellow food coloring to make the frosting orange. Frost the bottom layer, then lift the top layer on and frost the whole cake.

Make a jack-o' lantern face with candy bits, and sprinkle on a green sugar stem.

Caramel Apples
Everybody loves 'em!

You need:
4-5 red or green apples
1 package of caramels (with sticks included)
2 tablespoons water
Wax paper
Nuts, granola, or rice krispies if you like.

Wash and dry the apples. Twist off the stems. Insert a stick in each apple where the stem used to be. Put the caramels and 2 tablespoons of water in a pan on low heat. When the caramels are melted turn off the heat. Dip the apples in the pan, one at a time, holding them by the stick. Coat them well. Let the

Caramel Apples (cont.)

excess caramel sauce drip back into the pot. Roll the caramel apples into nuts, granola, or rice krispies, or leave them plain. Place on wax paper or foil to cool.

You can decorate your caramel apples to make great placecards. Cut out small pumpkins, witches, bats, ghosts, etc. (Draw your own or use magazine pictures). Write a guest's name on each shape. Tape it to the top of the stick. Your friends will have fun finding their places at the party table!

Ghost Pops

You need:
Tootsie pops
White tissues
Thread, string, yarn or ribbon
Black felt tip pen - with thin tip

Ghost pops are a good Halloween party favor for each guest. To make them, spread out a tissue, put a tootsie pop in the center, and wrap the tissue over the pop. Tie the pop with thread, string, yarn or ribbon. To make ghost eyes, dot lightly with marking pen.

Spider Web Game

You need a tangled up string with a prize on the end for each of your guests. To organize this, tie a party favor at the end of a ball of string or yarn. Hide the favor, then trail the string around tables, under chairs - in and out of things - as you unwind. Tie a pencil to the other end of the string, and also a card with a guest's name on it. Do this for each party guest, crisscrossing and tangling strings. Use different colors of yarn or string if you like. When your friends come they roll-up the string to find their prizes!

Witch Relay

Divide into 2 teams. (For more about teams and relays see p. 161). Give each team captain a broom and an object to sweep (such as a paper plate, peanut, old sock, rubber bat, etc.) Give each team the same kind of object to sweep. When a signal is given each team sweeps the object to the finish line and back until one team wins. To vary this game give each team a witch hat for the players to wear when sweeping. If the hat falls off, put it back on and keep going!

List of Costume Ideas

Here is a list of costume ideas in case you can't think of anything that appeals to you....

ghost
clown
pirate
witch
dragon
tiger
vampire
phantom
shark
Hobbit

butterfly
astronaut
robot
panda
star queen
scarecrow
watermelon
centipede
goldfish
ballerina

tooth fairy
famous person
vegetable
fruit
animal
zombi
owl
tree
dancer
musician

anything you want to be

Thanksgiving

Family Holidays
Turkey Napkin Holder

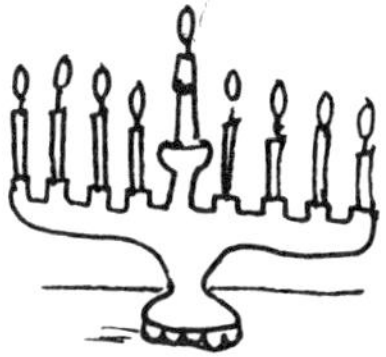

Thanksgiving, Christmas and Hanukkah are special family holidays. You can add to your family's celebration by making special foods and decorations.

Turkey Napkin Holder

To make a turkey napkin holder you need a small box or basket. Cut wings, feathers, head and feet from construction paper. Decorate with crayons, paints or marking pens and paste them on the box or basket. Roll up napkins and put them in your turkey holder. Good for nuts or candy too! Great centerpiece!

Turkey Placecards

Everyone will enjoy these turkeys that show them where to sit at the holiday table. Make a paper loop for the body and glue on a small paper loop head. Add a beak, eyes, wings and feet with scraps of bright paper. Glue a circle to the back of the body for the turkey's tail. You can feather the tail by cutting it  or decorate it by adding colored paper feathers. Colored magazine pictures make great feathers. Write a name on each turkey with a colored marking pen. Put a turkey behind each plate.

Hot Bacon Roll-Ups
Good holiday appetizers!

You need:

Refrigerated crescent rolls

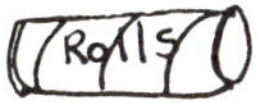

6 slices bacon or $\frac{1}{3}$ cup bacon bits

1 cup grated cheddar cheese

Adult help for frying if needed.

Makes 8 rolls.

Preheat oven to 375 degrees. Fry 6 slices of bacon until crisp. Drain and crumble on paper towels. Bacon bits can be used instead of fresh bacon. Grate cheese. Separate the crescent rolls and sprinkle each with cheese and bacon.
Roll up the dough, starting with the wide end.
Put on baking pan point side down. Bake at 375 degrees 12-15 minutes.

Ham and Cream Cheese Rolls

You need:
Sweet or dill pickle
1- 8 ounce package of cream cheese (at room temperature)
Boiled ham slices or sliced salami

Leave the cream cheese out of the refrigerator to let it soften. Salt it to taste. Cut the ham or salami slices in half. Dice pickles (cut them in small pieces). Mix the pickles with the cream cheese and spread the mixture on the lunch meat. Roll up the ham or salami slices and keep them in the refrigerator until you are ready to serve them. Add bits of parsley to the serving dish for a garnish.

Dutch Apple Muffins

You need:

- 1 egg
- 1/2 cup milk
- 1/4 cup cooking oil
- 1 1/2 cups flour
- 1/2 cup sugar
- 2 teaspoons baking powder
- 1/2 teaspoon salt
- 1/2 teaspoon cinnamon
- 1 medium-sized green apple, peeled, chopped in small bits (or sliced).

Preheat oven to 400 degrees. The secret to good muffins is not to overmix them. The batter should be lumpy. Break the egg in a big bowl and beat it slightly with a fork. Stir in the milk and oil. Measure other ingredients. Sift together flour, sugar, baking powder, salt, and cinnamon. Add this to the egg mixture. Add the chopped apples. Just stir a little! Put paper muffin cups in the muffin tin. Pour in batter. Bake 25-30 minutes at 400 degrees.

Hanukkah
Happy Hanukkah

Hanukkah Box

A Hanukkah Box will hold all the presents that you give and receive during Hanukkah. Get a large cardboard box. Cover it with tissue, wrapping paper, construction paper or foil. Decorate it with Hanukkah symbols. Put your presents inside the box.

How to Make a Dreidel
Playing the Dreidel Game

A dreidel is a 4-sided top. You can easily make one by cutting one section from a cardboard egg carton. Stick a short pencil through the center to make a top.  On each of 4 sides put one of the following Hebrew letters: נ nes ג gadol ה haya ש sham. These letters begin the words that mean "A great miracle happened here."

If you find the Hebrew letters difficult to make, you may want to use the letters N (nes), G (gadol), H (haya) and Sh (sham) instead. To play the dreidel game, give each player the same

Playing the Dreidel Game (cont.)

amount of coins, chips, toothpicks, nuts, candy, or any counter. Each player puts a counter in the "pot." Then each player takes a turn spinning the dreidel. If the dreidel stops at נ (N) the player takes nothing. If it stops at ג (G), he or she takes everything in the pot. If the dreidel stops at ה (H), the player takes half of what is in the pot. If it stops at ש (Sh), the player puts another counter in the pot. The winner is the person with the most counters. The game can be played for fun, or the winner can get a prize.

Potato Latkes (Pancakes)

Adult help may be needed for frying.

You need:
2 grated potatoes
2 eggs
1 teaspoon salt
1 heaping table-spoon flour
pinch of baking powder
1 small grated onion
Cooking oil
Frying pan, grater

Peel potatoes and grate them into a bowl. Peel the onion (don't cry), and grate it into the same bowl. Mix in other ingredients. Cover the bottom of the frying pan with oil. Heat it. Drop pancake mixture by the tablespoonful into the hot pan. This makes small pancakes. If you like thin, crisp latkes, flatten them with the back of a spoon. Fry on both sides until lightly browned. Good with applesauce, sour cream. Serves 4-6.

Cheese Rolls
Makes 12 Rolls

You need:
- 2 cups flour
- 2 teaspoons baking powder
- ½ teaspoon salt
- 1 egg, separated
- 1 cup milk
- ½ cup grated American or cheddar cheese
- Strainer or egg separator
- Muffin tin
- Paper muffin cups

Preheat oven to 400 degrees. Sift dry ingredients together into a bowl. To separate egg yolk from egg white, put a strainer over a cup and break the egg into it. (Or use an egg separator.) Put the yolk in a small bowl and beat it with a fork. Add beaten yolk and milk to dry ingredients. Beat 1 minute. Beat egg white until stiff. Add cheese and other ingredients to egg white, and mix lightly. Pour into muffin papers in muffin tin. Bake at 400 degrees for 20 minutes.

Hanukkah Sugar Cookies

You need:
- 4 sticks of butter or margarine (at room temperature)
- 2 cups sugar
- 2 teaspoons vanilla
- 5 cups flour

Preheat oven to 300 degrees. You can cut these sugar cookies into traditional Hanukkah shapes such as lions, Daniels, Judiths, stars, etc. Use cookie cutters or cardboard patterns.

In a large bowl beat together the butter, sugar and vanilla until it is well mixed. Beat in the flour until it is blended thoroughly and dough holds together. Roll out to $\frac{1}{4}$ inch thick on a floured board. Cut out and bake in 300 degree

Hanukkah Sugar Cookies (cont.)

oven for 25-30 minutes or until dough is pale gold and the center of the cookie is set when touched.

Paint On Frosting

Gradually add 6 tablespoons of water to a pound of powdered sugar. Add ½ teaspoon vanilla Mixture should flow smoothly but "set" quickly. Add more powdered sugar if necessary.

For colored frosting put frosting in small bowls and add food coloring. "Paint" frosting on cookies with a knife, spatula , or small, clean paintbrush.

Christmas

Sleigh Placecards

Use this tiny sleigh for placecards on the Christmas table. Cut the bottom sections of an egg carton apart.  Paint each section. (Red or green will look Christmassy). Bend pipe cleaners to look like runners on a sleigh.  Glue 2 runners to each egg cup. Fill the tiny sleighs with nuts, raisins, candy, or small toys. Write a name on each sleigh. This favor can also be used on your Christmas tree or packages.

Mobile Tree Centerpiece

You need 2 or 3 small tree branches (use dead branches that have fallen off a tree) and a large lump of clay to make a tree mobile. A flower "frog"  can be used instead of clay. Put the clay or frog at the bottom of a bowl or vase.

Stick the branches in and decorate them with all kinds of hanging ornaments - Santas, bells, stars, candy canes, small pine cones. Cover the vase or bowl with colored paper, fabric, netting, cotton, or holly or small Christmas tree branches. This tree will add a very special magic to your holiday table.

Christmas Cranberry Jello Mold

Make this the night before.

You need:
1 package Knox unflavored gelatin
2 - 3 ounce boxes orange jello
2 cups boiling water
1 cup cold water
1 - 16 ounce can solid cranberry sauce
1 - 20 ounce can crushed pine-apple, drained
Chopped nuts
3 quart jello mold

Mix 1 package of unflavored gelatin with $\frac{1}{4}$ cup cold water. In a large bowl mix the orange jello with 2 cups of boiling water. Stir the jello until it is completely dissolved. Add cranberry sauce and stir until it is in small pieces. Add the pineapple and the gelatin. Mix ingredients well. Add 1 cup cold water and mix well. Pour this mixture into the large

mold. Sprinkle chopped nuts on top of the jello. Put the mold in the refrigerator and let it set over-night. To unmold the jello, dip the bottom of the mold into warm water for a few seconds, or until you feel the jello loosening. (This happens quickly!) Place the serving plate on top of the mold, hold firmly, and flip over so that the jello goes onto the plate. Get help if necessary. If you like, decorate your jello with parsley.

Helpful hint: If your mold is not teflon, lightly grease it with a napkin and salad oil to make your jello easier to unmold.

Christmas Banners

Christmas banners are easy to make by cutting colored paper into a banner shape. Use fabric for a more elaborate banner. Add details with fabric or paper scraps. Hang your banner on a pole, wooden dowel, or colored strip of paper. Add bells, stars, tassels, or other trims. For an extra special banner use felt.

Gingerbread Kids

Make other shapes too if you like.

You need:		
1 cup shortening	1 cup molasses	1 tablespoon ginger
1 cup sugar	2 tablespoons vinegar	1 teaspoon cinnamon
½ teaspoon salt	5 cups flour	1 teaspoon cloves
1 egg	1½ teaspoons soda	

Cream (blend) shortening, sugar and salt in a large bowl. Stir in egg, molasses, and vinegar and beat well. Sift together the dry ingredients in another bowl. Stir

them into the molasses mixture. Chill the dough for about 3 hours. Then take $\frac{1}{3}$ of the dough at a time. Sprinkle flour on a board and roll the dough to $\frac{1}{8}$ inch thick. Cut with cookie cutters. Place 1-inch apart on a greased cookie sheet. Bake at 375 degrees for 6 minutes. Cool and remove from pan. Decorate with icing-in-a-tube, raisins, red hot candies, whatever you like. You can add names too. Wrap in plastic wrap and tie with colorful ribbons to hang them on a tree!

Santa Claus Piñata

A piñata is easy to make from wrapping paper. Cut 2 "teardrop" shapes the size you want the piñata. This will make Santa's face and hat. Cut pink and red tissue paper into 3-inch strips. Cut and fringe each strip. Start at the bottom of one paper, and glue on pink fringe. Put the next tissue above the first one. Continue layering until you get about 2/3 of the way

Santa Claus Piñata (cont.)

up the face. 

Now switch to red tissue for Santa's hat. Add eyes, nose and mouth of colored paper. Tear white tissue for the beard and mustache. Cover the other red teardrop with red tissue, starting at the bottom. Staple the 2 papers together at the sides, fringe side out. Fill your piñata with wrapped candy, gum, peanuts, toys. Staple it closed and hang it!

To break the piñata, blindfold one person at a time, twirl him or her around, and let him or her try to break it with a stick ¡olé!

Valentine's
Day

Valentines Day

Heart streamers made from crepe paper are a colorful Valentine decoration. Hang all kinds of hearts of different sizes and colors. Make heart animals, people, designs, flowers – or just plain hearts.

Banners are a good decoration too. Just paste all kinds of hearts on paper or fabric, and hang the banner up.

Valentines Party Invitation

To make this invitation fold red, pink, or white paper in thirds.

Trace or draw a heart on your paper. Cut it out, leaving edges uncut along both folds. This way you will have a string of three hearts.

Write your invitation and fold the hearts closed so that the left-hand heart is on top. Decorate.

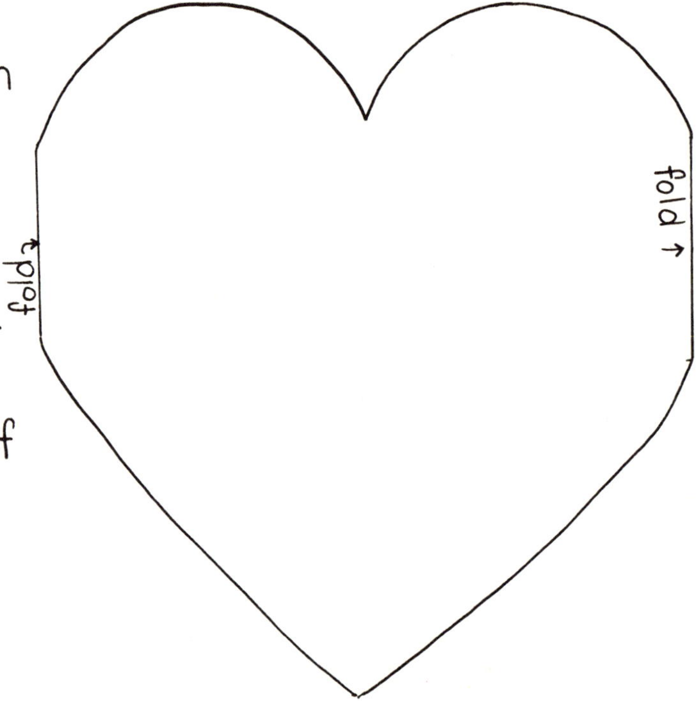

Crazy Heart Cake

You need:
Cake mix or your favorite cake recipe
Prepared frosting or frosting recipe
Assorted candies such as nonpareils, chocolate bits, M & M's, gumdrops, sprinkles, jelly beans, red hots, candy hearts, nuts.

Make your cake. Bake it and let it cool. Use a square or rectangular cake pan, or a heart-shaped pan if you have one. Frost the cake. Draw a big heart shape on the frosting with a toothpick. If your cake is heart-shaped, draw a smaller heart on the cake.

♡ Arrange your candies in small piles so you can see what you have. Put them on the cake. Outline the heart with candy hearts. Have fun!

Valentine Box
For Valentines or for a "Grab-Box"

If you are having your guests bring valentines, you will need a Valentine Box. The Valentine Box could also be a "grab-box" for your guests to reach in and pull out a surprise party favor!

Decorate a cardboard box with crepe paper and construction paper. Add hearts, lace, paper doilies, ribbons, cupids, arrows- things you like. Cut a slit in the top big enough to put your hand in. This box is a good way to pass out valentines or give your friends a special party favor!

Valentine Holder

This holder is for your friends to use to take home their valentines. Use 12 by 18 construction paper. Fold it in half. Draw a heart on it and cut it out. Do not cut on the fold.

Unfold the heart.

Fold the bottom heart up about ¼ of the way.

Trim edges.

Fold the bottom up and staple or glue the sides. This is a perfect pocket for carrying valentines home!

HAPPY
EASTER

Easter Egg Hunt

There are many different ways to organize an Easter Egg Hunt. You can hide hard-boiled, candy or paper eggs. Let your friends "trade-in" paper eggs for candy eggs or jelly beans, or give a prize to the one who collects the most eggs. If you hide real eggs you can wrap one egg in foil and give a prize for the silver egg. Another idea is to give each color a value - 5 for red, 4 for blue, etc. Write the points on the egg. Give a prize for the highest score.

Easter Egg Card
or Invitation

Fold a piece of paper in half. Draw an egg or trace this pattern.  Cut the egg out or leave it on the card. Be sure not to cut the fold. 

Decorate with crayons or marking pens. Write your message inside the egg.

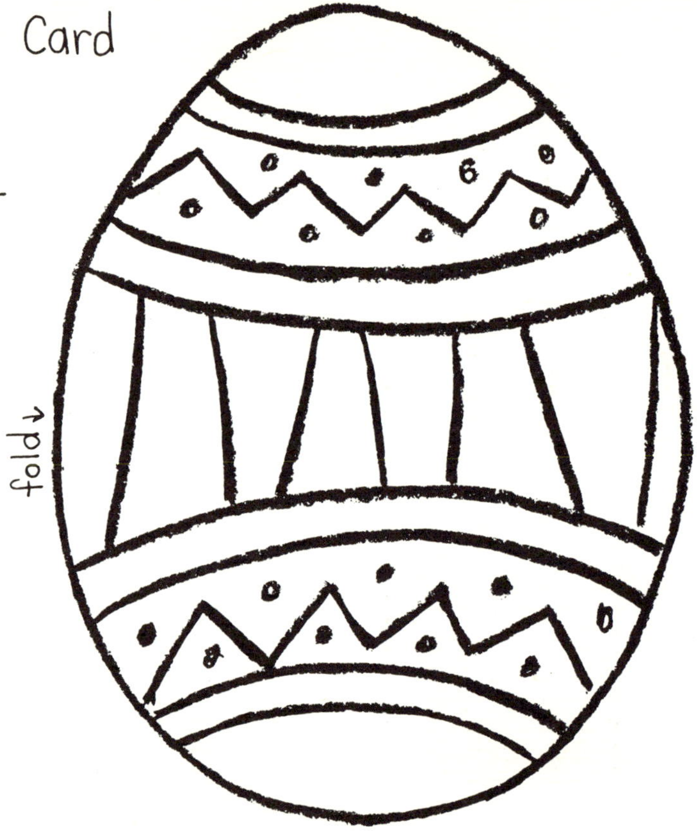

Egg Roll or Peanut Push

Push with nose

An Egg Roll is fun at Easter or any time. Have guests line up at a starting line with a hard-boiled egg or a peanut. When a signal is given, everyone tries to get the egg or peanut to the finish line first. Make this game a relay if you like. No hands!*

Egg Race

Set up two teams for an Egg Relay race. A player from each team takes a turn to run with an egg (hard-boiled!) on a spoon. You could also use a potato. Pick it up and keep going if it falls off!

* For more about relays see p. 161.

Cake of the Kings

This is a cake that can "tell your fortune." Mix your favorite cake recipe or mix. Before you bake it add small metal (<u>not</u> plastic!) charms. Or you can add fortunes you have written on small pieces of paper and rolled up tightly. Also add one dried bean.

Some metal charms you could use are a ring (whoever gets this in the slice of cake will marry ??) a thimble, a button, a coin, etc. Make up your own fortunes or meanings that go with each charm. Be sure the charms are clean before you put them in the cake batter. Try to add enough charms or fortunes so that everyone gets one in his or her slice of cake. (Or make cupcakes with a surprise in each one!)

Now for the special event! The person who gets the dried bean is crowned King or Queen of the Fiesta! (Make the crown ahead of time. See p.22).

Easter Bunny's Coffee Can Bread

You need:

1 package dry yeast
$\frac{1}{2}$ cup warm water
$\frac{1}{8}$ teaspoon ground ginger
3 tablespoons sugar
1-13 ounce can evaporated milk
1 teaspoon salt
2 tablespoons salad oil
4-4$\frac{1}{2}$ cups flour
Electric mixer and adult help if needed.

Dissolve yeast in warm water in a mixing bowl. Blend in ginger and 1 tablespoon of sugar. Let it stand in a warm place until mixture is bubbly. (About 15 minutes.) Stir in the rest of the sugar, and the milk, salt and salad oil. Beat in 3 cups of flour 1 cup at a time with an electric mixer. (Get help mixing if necessary.

Easter Bunny's Coffee Can Bread (cont.)

Beat in the rest of the flour by hand, with a wooden spoon. Beat until the dough is stiff.

Put a little salad oil or margarine on a piece of paper towel, and grease a clean 2-pound coffee can (or 2 1-pound cans). Grease the outer top inch of the can too. Place dough in can. Cover with plastic lids until bread dough reaches the top. (About 30 to 45 minutes.) Remove plastic lid. Preheat the oven to 350 degrees. Bake bread 45-60 minutes. Fresh baked bread is a special Easter treat!

Cascarones

Cascarones are confetti-filled egg shells. In Mexico cascarones are part of the fun at festivals and carnivals. People enjoy decorating the eggs - then they have fun breaking them over the heads of friends and family members. To make a Cascaron (confetti egg), break a small opening in each end of an egg. (Use a pin, then enlarge the holes slightly). Blow into the egg shell and let the egg drain into a

Cascarones (cont.)

dish. (Use it in cooking.) Rinse the egg shell and let it dry. Draw crayon designs or pictures or leave it plain. Color the egg in egg dye or food coloring.

When the egg shell is dry, fill it about $\frac{1}{3}$ full of confetti or cut up colored tissue . Seal the holes with tape, or glue on paper circles. Add fringe if you like. To make fringe cut 3 inch wide strips of tissue. Fold them and cut (fringe) the folded edge. Turn strips inside out and glue the uncut edges together, making a puffy fringe. Glue strips on the egg shell.

glue here for puffy fringe

Mothers' Day
Fathers' Day

Mother's Day Party Sandwiches

Mix fillings for a variety of sandwiches, or have lunch meats ready. Cut the crusts off the bread. (Save them for bread crumbs for another recipe.) Spread the bread with butter, mustard, mayonnaise — whatever Mom likes. Add lettuce, and lunch meats or fillings. Cut the sandwiches in triangles, rectangles or squares. →

Put on a tray. Decorate with parsley or a flower. (No bugs, please!)

You need:
Bread
Lunch meats or fillings, such as tuna, deviled ham, egg salad, chicken salad, chopped olives — Think of the foods Mom likes best!

Mother's Day Surprise Cake

Preheat oven to 350 degrees.

You need:

2 eggs
1 cup flour
$\frac{1}{2}$ cup milk and
1 tablespoon butter, warmed until butter melts
$\frac{1}{4}$ teaspoon salt
1 cup sugar
1 teaspoon baking powder
1 teaspoon vanilla
Egg beater or electric mixer + adult
8 by 8 inch cakepan

Beat eggs in a bowl and add sugar. Beat until the mixture is a pale lemon color. Sift the flour, salt, and baking powder together. Add it to the egg mixture. Add the milk, butter, vanilla. Stir the batter and pour it into an 8 by 8 inch cakepan. Bake at 350 degrees for 35 minutes.

When the cake is cool, cut it in half.  Spread jam on bottom half. Put other half on top. Sift powdered sugar on the top of your cake.

Mother's Day Card
A good Father's Day Card too!

It's fun to use old photographs to make very personal cards for Mom (or Dad). Draw a picture of your Mom doing something she likes to do. Cut out the face from the photograph and glue it on. Or glue on the entire cut photo and draw the background.

Dad's Brunch

Start this the night before!

Cut the crusts off the bread.* Butter the bread. Cut it into 1-inch cubes. Grease the pan, and put the bread cubes in it. Add cheese and cooked meat. Beat the eggs in a bowl. Add milk and salt. Pour this over the cheese-bread-meat mixture. Cover this and leave it in the refrigerator overnight. The next morning uncover, and bake for 1 hour at 350 degrees. This recipe serves 4. Double it to serve more people.

* Save crusts for another recipe.

You need:

5 slices bread, buttered

¼ pound cheddar cheese, shredded

½ pound bacon <u>or</u> ham, cooked and diced (this is about 8 slices bacon)

3 eggs

1½ cups milk

¼ teaspoon salt

Pyrex pan (about 8 by 8 inches)

Father's Day Card

Fold paper in half and cut an oval like an old-fashioned frame.

Trace this oval if you like. Draw a picture of your dad inside the frame. Write a note to your Dad on the inside of the card. Let him know the good things you think about him! This is a good idea for Mother's Day too!

12
Games

Organizing Party Games
Choosing "It"

Plan your party games ahead. Have all the equipment needed for each game ready before the party starts. Have prizes if you like.

There are several ways to choose someone to be "It". One way is to have your friends "draw" straws, cut toothpicks or paper strips. The person who gets the shortest one is "It". You can also have your friends pick the number you are thinking of from 1-10 or 1-25. (Write it down ahead of time to be fair!)

Choosing "It" (cont.)
Game Grab Bag too.

Counting rhymes are another way to pick "It". A good one is —"Eeny, meeny, miny, mo, catch a monster by the toe. If it hollers let it go, eeny, meeny, miny, mo!" Another rhyme is "ABCDEFGHI." (I is "It".)

If you like, have a Game Grab Bag, with the names of games planned written on paper strips. A guest picks a strip, and that is the next game played. (Be prepared to play games listed in the Grab Bag!)

Hunts

Hunts are a great way to begin a party! Before your guests arrive hide lots of surprises all over the room (more than enough for everyone). Give each guest a bag to put things in. The surprises you hide depend partly on the season. Some ideas are: Valentine's Day - candy hearts, real valentines; St. Patrick's Day - green candy, paper shamrocks; Easter - jelly beans, paper or real eggs; Halloween - candy corn, candy or paper pumpkins; Thanksgiving - peanuts, cut-out turkeys; Christmas or Hanukkah - small wrapped party favors with each child's name on them.

Pin the Tail on the Donkey (and Variations)

Pin the Tail on the Donkey is a favorite party game. Buy or draw a donkey and some donkey tails. Give each player a tail with his or her name on it, and a pin or tape. Blindfold and spin one player at a time. Give each a turn to pin or tape the tail in the right place. The person who gets the tail closest wins.

Some variations of this game are: Pin the Nose on the Witch (or on the Clown, Santa or Rudolph) draw whiskers on the Dog, Cat or Easter Rabbit, pin the Hat on a Leprechaun, Pin a Trunk on the Elephant, etc.

Giant Steps
Or Baby Steps, or Scissors Steps, or...

One player is the "Mother," who stands at the finish line. Other players are lined up at the starting line. "Mother" calls out the name of the first player and says something like, "Pam, you may take 2 giant steps." Pam says, "Mother, may I?" and takes the steps. If a player forgets to say "Mother, may I?", then he or she must stay in the same place until next turn. The first player to reach "Mother" is "Mother" in the next game.

Dog, Dog, the Bone!

Players sit in a circle. The player who is "It" (the Dog) sits in the center of the circle with eyes shut, head resting on arms. No peeking! The "bone" (any object), is on the floor behind the dog. One player is motioned (by whoever is supervising the game) to steal the bone. When this player gets back in the circle all players put their arms behind their backs. Then everyone says "Dog, dog, where's your bone?" The Dog gets 3 guesses. Whether the dog guesses correctly or not, the player who took the bone is the next Dog.

Hot Potato
Button, Button too.

Players sit in a circle and pass a potato, ball or other object while music is playing. When the music stops, the player holding the potato is out. Keep going until one player is left. He or she is the winner!

Button, Button

Players sit in a circle with one person ("It") in the middle. Players pass a button around the circle, keeping their arms moving constantly. "It" tries to guess who has the button. When "It" guesses, he or she trades places with the button-holder.

Drop the Clothespin

For this game you need clothespins, and a jar, bottle or milk carton with the top opened up. A jar or bottle will make the game more exciting. Give each player a turn to see how many clothespins he or she can drop in the bottle. No bending over! The one who gets the most clothespins in the bottle wins.

To vary the game use lollipops or peanuts instead of clothes-pins.

Fishing

You need a fish pole (or a stick with a string) and a small toy or party favor for each guest. You also need an adult or other friend to tie on a gift for each guest.

Hang a sheet or crepe paper to section off a "Fish Pond". Have your friends take turns putting the fishing line into the pond. With the help of the person behind the curtain, everyone will pull out a surprise! One favor to a customer!

Make a Basket
Discus Throw too.

You need a wastebasket and balls, bean-bags, or other objects. Have each player stand behind a line. Everyone gets 3 chances to make a basket. This is a good relay too!

Discus Throw

Give each player a paper plate. See who can throw it the farthest. To vary the game see who can throw it the highest, roll it the farthest, etc.

Red Light, Green Light

Players line up on a starting line. A leader stands at the finish line with his or her back to the group. When the leader says "Green Light" everyone walks or runs toward the finish line. At short intervals the leader calls "Red Light" and turns around fast. When they hear "Red Light" the players must "freeze" in the positions they are in. Anyone caught moving goes back to the start. The first one to reach the leader is "It".

Relay Races

Relay Races are exciting games! Play them outdoors if you can, or in a big room. Relays are played in teams (usually 2 teams for up to 16 or 20 players, 3 or 4 teams for a larger group). Try to have the same number of players on a team. If a team is short a player, the leader must run first and last.

Number off 1-2, 1-2-3, or 1-2-3-4, to pick the number of teams you need. Have teams line up on a starting line with one player behind the other. Leave space

Ideas for Relays

between teams. When someone gives the signal "Go", the first player from each team runs to a finish line (or does whatever is required for that relay). Each leader goes back and tags the second player on the team, then goes to the end of the line. When everyone on a team has had a turn, the leader is at the front of the line again. The first team finished wins.

Some good relays are: running, hopping, skipping, jumping (forward or backward), or a combination of any of these. Other ideas are overhead ball pass, underlegs ball pass, between

legs ball roll, book on head relay, rope skipping relay, hopping with a cup of water, hopping inside a sack (Sack Race), roll the hoop or tire relay, etc. There are other relay ideas on the next 3 pages.

Old Clothes or Costume Relay

Give each team a box or suitcase full of things to wear. Some ideas are: gloves, hats, scarves, aprons, big shoes - anything easy to put on. The first players carry the box to the goal, put everything on, rush to the start and put everything back in the box. The next player does the same thing. First team finished wins.

Pop the Balloon Relay
Crawling Relay too.

For this relay you need a blown-up balloon for each player, and a chair at the finish line for each team. At the signal, the first player from each team runs to the chair with a balloon and sits on the balloon until it pops. The player then runs back and tags the next player.

Crawling Relay

The first player from each team turns to face his or her team. At the word, "Go", the players crawl under the legs of teammates to the end of the line, then stand up. Then the next player goes, until everyone has had a turn.

Chinese Hop

For this relay you need 2 teams and 2 sets of sticks (popsicle sticks, twigs, rulers, etc.). Each team places the sticks in a row about 18 inches apart. Be sure there is a stick for each player on a team.

When the signal is given, the first player on each team hops on one foot over every stick, picks up the last stick, hops back and tags the next player. The first team to pick up all of its sticks wins the game.

Three-Legged Race

Pair off your friends and have each team of 2 tie their inside legs together with rope or string. Everyone runs in pairs to the goal. Takes teamwork!

Sack Race

This game can be a relay or a race with everyone lined up on a starting line. Each player stands in gunny sack, holds onto it and hops to the goal.

Snake Race

"Snakes" of 4-6 players are formed. Everyone holds on and the "snake" runs to a goal. Good relay too!

Tag and Variations of Tag

In a basic game of tag, one player is "It" and tries to tag the other players. Anyone caught is "It".

Duck Tag

Players can run around, but must squat like a duck to avoid being tagged.

Shadow Tag

The player who is "It" tries to step on a shadow (or a certain part of the shadow, such as the head) to tag someone. Can only be played on a sunny day.

Surprise Ball Game

Make a Surprise Ball (see p. 69) with lots of party favors in different layers inside. Have your guests sit in a circle and pass the ball around as the music plays. When the music stops the person holding the ball gets to unwind it until a party favor is discovered (which he or she gets to keep). Start the music and pass the ball again. Keep going until the last favor has been found. Try to have the person in charge of the music time the stopping of the music in such a way that everyone gets a favor.

Sardines

If you play this game you could end up as squashed as sardines in a can! Choose one player to be "It". This player is the Sardine. The Sardine hides. Other players close their eyes and count to 100, then look for the Sardine. If a player finds the Sardine then he or she hides there too. It can get pretty crowded! (And hard not to laugh!) The game continues until everyone is hiding in the same place. The last player to find the others is the next Sardine.

Shoe Scramble

Simon Says too.

Have players mark their initials on the bottoms of their shoes, and put them in a pile across the room. At the word "Go", players race to put on their shoes and be the first ones back to the starting line (in the right shoes!)

Simon Says

Choose Simon, who gives orders to the other players, such as "Simon says jump 2 times." Players must obey only when they hear the words "Simon says." Anyone who does something without hearing "Simon says" is out. The player who stays in the game the longest is the new Simon.

Heavy, Heavy Hangs Over Your Head- A Forfeit Game

Pick 2 people to be "It", a judge and a leader. The other players each put something of their own in a box- a shoe, shoelace, ribbon, etc. The judge is then blind-folded. The leader picks one object at a time from the box and holds it over the judge's head saying "Heavy, heavy hangs over your head. What shall the owner do to redeem it?" The judge (who does not know what the object is or who owns it) assigns a forfeit that the person must pay to get the object back. The judge can make up any silly stunt. See forfeit ideas on p. 173.

A List of Forfeits and Silly Stunts

Pretend to be a wild pig
Push peanuts across the room with your nose
Jump like a frog
Dance with a broom
Lap up a saucer of milk
Eat a cracker and try to whistle
Spell your name backwards
Be a bucking broncho
Hold your nose and sing
Be an animal
Jump across the room with an inflated balloon between your knees. (Don't pop it!)
Jump rope backwards
Grab your ankles and walk like a duck
Be a caged gorilla
Imitate a jet
Tell a riddle
Carry a book on your head
Anything else you think of...

HELPING OUT PARTIES

Helping Out Parties

One of the nicest parties you can have is one where you and your friends work together to help other people.

One of the things you can do is to make cards, perfume sachets, small gifts or baked goodies for older people in convalescent hospitals. You could also collect magazines, clothing, or books for an orphanage or hospital. Collect toys or games too. Take these to your local police or fire department for repair and distribution.

Helping Out Parties (cont.)

Another thing you can do is to put on a play, puppet show or musical event for a hospital, orphanage or home for older people. Call up the director or whoever is in charge to make your plans and set a show time.

You may have more ideas about how to help someone-maybe through a church or community group. Ask adults to help you plan. You will bring a lot of pleasure to others!

Ideas for Excursion Parties

You and your family may decide to take your friends somewhere, rather than have your party at home. Choices depend upon what is available in your area (and on your budget, of course). Here are some suggestions of places to go:

- Pizza Parlor
- Ice Cream Parlor
- Ice Skating
- Roller Skating
- Amusement Park
- City Park
- Zoo
- Movie
- Boat, subway, train or bus ride
- Ball Game
- Circus
- Tea Garden

Index

Introducing Young Artists

Nitty Gritty Productions appreciates the artistic efforts of the following young artists whose drawings appear in this book.

Michelle Bissell Next to Title Page
Jose Casas p. 78
Yvonne Cauchi pp. 26, 88
Teresa Collett p. 165
Heidi Guttormsen p. 132
Kathy Hall p. 64
Sergio Huerta p. 148
Marcus Mayer Last Page in Book
Roxanne Maynard p. 84
Chris Mayorga p. 174
Claire McGhee p. 70
Eva Marie McNeil pp. 48, 108
Kimberly Mikkelson p. 33
Rena Mikkelson First Page in Book
Monica Nelson p. 38
Omar Oceguera p. 157
Cathleen Petrich pp. 102, 142
Tanya Pavloff p. 56
Elaine Saldanha p. 11
Teri Valadez p. 116
Rod Walsh pp. 15, 126
Preston Ward p. 95
Margarita Wien Next to Introduction